Seasonal Foraging:
15 Wild Plants To Find In The Forest

Table of content

Introduction: Living off the Land and the Edibility Test

Before you attempt to eke out any sustenance from the land you need to first take stock of the natural environment. And if you are like 54% of our planet's increasingly urbanized population, you are probably more used to an urban environment. And that being said, your senses are probably very out of sync with the natural world. Your sense of smell—one of the most important senses you can use when foraging for wild food—has most likely been dulled by all of those years of city life.

Decades of smog has most of us city dwellers with a greatly diminished scent capacity. And besides the actual affects of pollutants on our nostrils, those of us that live in urban environs, instead of learning to use our ability of smell as a discerning tool, have learned to block many of the oppressive odors of closed space humanity out. We have learned not to take in the fragrance of the air, because we're used to it not being quite so pleasant in the first place.

When foraging however we need to learn how to bring our power of smell back online, because detecting a strong fragrance from a plant is the first step in what's known as the "edibility test" when it comes to foraging wild foods in the great outdoors. Before eating anything you find growing wild you should take a good whiff of the plant and pay special attention to see if it is emitting any strong odors, especially acidic odors.

Next to scent, another way to test out a plant you are unsure of is to take the whole plant and then break it down into its most basic components. Break it down piece by piece, to its flowers, buds, roots, stems, and leaves. This is very important, because some plants may have poisonous flowers, and others may have poisonous roots, buds, stems or leaves.

At first glance there is just no way of knowing for sure, this is why you must break it all down by individual section. After you have done this; on an empty stomach place a small piece of each section of the plant on your wrist. This is a sensitive part of your skin and after pressing it to your wrist for about 15 minutes, if the plant is poisonous you would probably get some sort of reaction—possibly numbness or a tingling sensation—from absorbing a trace amount of the toxic element.

This is why it's so much safer to test a plant's chemical makeup by putting it up against your skin rather than ingesting it. Because even if a plant is poisonous, the small amount absorbed by the skin, can't do any serious damage. It would be just enough to get a brief reaction. But ingesting even a small piece of a plant poses a much more serious risk since you are consuming it internally where you can't easily get rid of it and a larger amount of the chemical is rapidly absorbed into the stomach.

But hold on a second, because the skin test is only the first step in our testing process, to really be thorough, after the skin test we are going to put the plant piece up to our lips and hold it there for another 15 minutes, if there still isn't a reaction, then you can go ahead and put it in your mouth. But don't swallow it, just leave it on your tongue for an additional 15 minutes and then spit it out.

After this little spit test, if you are then still confident that you are not feeling any ill effects such as burning, itching or any other discomfort you can then take a slightly bigger piece and chew it for—you guessed it—15 minutes. If you are still feeling pretty good after chewing your plant material you can then go on to the step of actually swallowing it.

Now for the final part of the edibility test, don't eat anything else for about 8 hours, you can see now why it was specified to begin the testing process on an empty stomach. Just a means of classic scientific control in our experiment to make sure that any negative reaction you have is from the wild food and not the (semi-wild) Taco Bell burrito you had for lunch!

And so with your new found plant material nicely isolated in the experimental petri dish of your stomach, closely monitor your condition over the next 8 hours. If you do have the misfortune of suddenly starting to feel sick you should try drinking a lot of water and induce vomiting immediately to eject all of the plant from your system.

But if no ill effects occur after your eight hour period, you should be on easy street, and can pat yourself on the back for adding a brand new plant species to your arsenal of wild foods to forage. It may be repetitive, and at times it may even seem silly, but these are just some of the steps that you have to take if you truly want to live off the land.

Chapter 1: Springtime Foraging

Spring is a wonderful time of year in which everything seems to be coming to life. Flowers are in bloom, and the air is abuzz with energy and promise. And as you may have guessed, spring is a very promising time to forage. This chapter goes down the list of some of the best wild foods of spring.

Dandelion

Dandelions are known as both a weed and a flower, and although it originally took root in Europe, it has spread to North America and beyond. This wild food is in season beginning in April and typically last well into June. The stems of the Dandelion are very nutritious and can serve as a great dietary supplement.

You can boil them in a soup, make them part of a salad or just eat them by themselves. But while it is the stem of this plant that provides a great source of nutrition, it is the root of this wild food that many have sworn by, because the roots of this wild food can be used to make great brews of both coffee and beer.

Burdock

Closely related to the dandelion is the wild growing Burdock plant, and consequently enough it can be made into some hardy beer as well! Many blends of Burdock beer even mix the roots of this plant with dandelions to achieve a great tasting and powerful drink. Just add some sugar and yeast and you have the makings of a fantastic brew.

And besides drinking blends made from their roots, actually eating the roots works out pretty good too, just cut up the Burdock's roots into matchstick sized pieces and then fry them up in a pan for about 20 minutes and you will have yourself some tasty Burdock stir fry!

Burdock root is best dug up early in the spring season, right around March or April. The leaves of the Burdock are edible too but they may taste a bit bitter and you have to be sure to remove the cordage wrapped around them first before trying to eat them. This plant is easily spotted by its kidney shaped leaves and the purplish blue color of their flowers.

Stinging Nettle

Despite the name, the Stinging Nettle is a fairly pleasant wild food to eat. These plants shoot right up in the spring time and are usually found in dark rich soil. During the spring season the shoots of the plant can be about 3 or 4 inches tall and are an excellent source of vegetation. They work well in soups, stews, or in salads. You can also save the dried leaves for later use and even use them to make a fairly tasty tea.

Nutrition wise, the Nettle is a real boon too, since it is naturally high in calcium, silicon, potassium, phosphorous and iron. If you are unable to get your calcium through milk due to lactose intolerance or because you are getting your nourishment solely through the wild food you forage, this plant can be a great calcium supplement. As mentioned, the plant is also so chocked full of iron I have known people that were Iron anemic who took this plant to balance out the iron in their blood. All of thee reasons make the spring time Nettle a great addition to your wild food supply.

Hawthorn

This wild food begins to make its presence known in the opening months of spring as it begins to grow edible leaves, buds and berries. The flower buds and leaves are an excellent ingredient in salads and the berries are good by themselves or can be mixed into an excellent jam that you can seal up in a jar and save for later.

The leaves of the Hawthorne plant also be used for tea, but be careful before you drink it, because there have been a rare few that have had allergic reactions to it. So maybe just sample a bit before you determine whether or not you have a good tolerance to it. Spring is a season when the whole world comes to life just take the time to take it all in as you forage for your wild foods.

Chapter 2: Summer Harvest

The summer harvest has arrived! The summer is a great time of year and as the land heats up you can find a virtual smorgasbord of wild food to choose from. Here are a few that you should look out for.

Wild Violets

One of the best groupings of wild food to forage during the summer months are plants in the violet family. These plants bloom between May and August and can be found everywhere from inside the reaches of dense forest, to making cameo appearances in your own backyard. So let's take a look at some of the best wild fauna that the summer months have to offer.

When you pick a violet from the ground you are collecting a truly edible plant, because every part of these wild flowers can be eaten, from the tip of their roots, to their leaves, and the petals of their flowers. The leaves of the plant make for an excellent salad or stand alone veggie. This wild food is a great source of Vitamin A as well as Vitamin C, taking care of two of the body's most important nutrition requirements in just this one wild plant.

Wild Strawberries

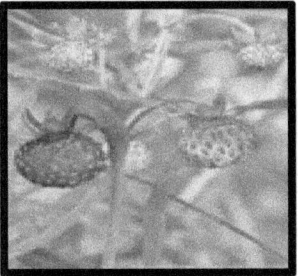

These tasty wild treats start popping up in open woodland and even open fields (Does the Beatles 'Strawberry Fields Forever' come to mind?) These wild berries usually make their appearance right around the beginning of July, making them firmly in the summer category for foraging. Wild strawberries look very similar to the kind you find on the store shelves they are just usually smaller in size.

Many people are afraid to eat Wild Strawberries because they are afraid that they are poisonous, but wild strawberries are just as safe as store bought strawberries. Just make sure that you don't misidentify this wild food with some of its less edible cousins. The first visual cue that the wild strawberry will give you is the distinctive white coloring of the wild strawberry flower which first begins to bloom around May. When you see these white flowers appearing in one or more clusters you can be sure that their red colored strawberries are not far behind.

Wild Blueberries

Just like wild strawberries this wild food is at its height of growth in the middle of July. Wild Blueberries tend to congregate in woody shrub areas and especially likes the meadow soil of the Canadian Shield. But they have also been found randomly growing in vacant lots, parks, and even in some cases; backyards. These wild blueberries are best eaten raw. But if you really want to cook them they can also serve you well as a dried additive in bread and cakes. Wild Blueberry Muffin anyone?

Chapter 3: Fall Leaves, Nuts, Seeds and Weeds

For a lot of people fall is their favorite time of year, and I understand why. Because as the summer draws to a close and the long days finally get cooler and begin to shorten, we naturally find ourselves beginning to relax. But as the leaves begin to fall, some of the best in wild forage fauna begins to arrive.

Purslane

This wild plant is believed to have originated in the Mid East, but since ancient times it has traveled the world and has its toe hold in just about every part of the planet. During the summer months you can find this wild food just about everywhere, but in my experience over here in North America, I most often find this wild one growing in the cracks of sidewalks than anywhere else.

For some reason it seems to like the structure that pavement provides, and since this plant grows flat rather than upright, it can quickly spread all over the place. Considered little more than a common weed nuisance by some, this plant is unmistakable with its thick red stems and oval shaped leaves. Although many frown upon this plant for its ability to rapidly multiple all over the place, they may want to start singing the tune of, "If you can't beat them... Eat them!"

Because these guys are packed with all kinds of nutrients, in fact, just one stem of Purslane typically comes loaded with Omega 3, Vitamin A, Vitamin E, Calcium, Phosphorus and a whole boatload of healthy carbohydrates and fatty acids; all things our body needs. As you can see, Purslane is one of nature's original multi-vitamins. So if you are trying to rough it over the summer, foraging for this prevalent plant could do you a lot of good.

American Shamrock

For our next wild food, we are going to borrow the luck of the Irish to forage for our very own American Shamrock. Easily identifiable by its iconic, clovered, shamrock shape, this wild plant is edible cooked or raw. This wild food has a very fresh taste and is great in salad or veggie platters. The plant is usually about 6 inches in height and is usually found taking up space on sunny lawns and sidewalks. There is also a woodland variety of this Shamrock that usually has white or pink flowers.

Every single part of this plant is edible but take this one warning however, since the Shamrock contains a lot of oxalic acid, it is best taken in moderation, since consuming too much of this wild food has been known to lead to kidney stones. And let me tell you! If you have ever had to pump a kidney stone out of your body, you certainly don't feel lucky! No matter how many shamrocks you ate!

Acorns

This is a wild food I used to love as a kid. Every fall me and the other neighborhood kids would go and gather them as they scattered all over the ground. Acorns are certainly a great find while you are foraging just be sure you rinse them off, or even better yet gather a bucket of them and let them soak overnight. You want to do this to take off some of the bitter taste that lingers on their exterior. With a good rinse job however, the bitterness can be completely washed away. These guys can then be eaten either in their natural state or perhaps ground up into powder and then fried as tasty acorn cakes.

Mustard Seeds

The wild mustard plant from which the mustard seed is harvest really comes into its own between the Fall months of September and October. Mustard plants are found usually in wide open fields that get a lot of sunshine. This is another wild food that it is good to have a nose for when you are foraging because it has a very distinctive odor. Once you know the smell of wild mustard you don't forget it.

The flowers of the mustard plant are either yellow or white in a 4 petal layout, usually in an X kind of shape. The seedpods are shaped like little hearts and with these the seeds form a kind of spiral like staircase ascending up the stem. The seeds taste great by themselves as a snack, as a garnishment on top of a salad, and can even be made into its very own wild food version of conventional mustard (As in ketchup and mustard). The Fall season just got a whole lot better with these wild foods!

Chapter 4: Gathering The Last Foods of Winter

Winter is a magical time of year. If you live far enough north, the snow is falling, lakes are freezing and birds are migrating. And if you are trying to provide for yourself by foraging through the winter months, you may feel like you are suddenly hard pressed to find any wild plants. But although winter brings a lot of change in the environment, for a resourceful forager, there is still plenty of wild food on the horizon.

Watercress

This wild winter food is similar in consistency to lettuce and makes for a delicious winter time salad. It can often be found nestled amid bright green shrubbery near water. Since this wild food is positioned near water it is very important for you to make sure that the water source that this plant is living off of is not contaminated by industrial waste. Unfortunately this has become a major problem in many parts of the world, so once again, having a good awareness of the environment in which you forage is a big plus when it comes to Watercress.

Chickweed

This delicious wild food is easily spotted when its star shaped flower shoots up out of the snow. During the winter season they are usually found in wide open areas where the sun has melted down the snow a bit, revealing patches of these Chickweeds in the grass. These open patches often emerge through snow trails, and heavily trod foot paths. Basically anywhere that the snow has melted and the ground has been opened up a bit, you will find this wild food.

Oyster Mushrooms

Finally! There is a fungus among us! Oyster Mushrooms are a tasty treat and a nice way to break up your foraging monotony. These mushrooms are also extremely prevalent during the winter months. One of the most common places to find this wild food is on a fallen log in a snow bank. No matter how cold it is you can see the telltale sign of this fungi's mushroom cap sticking up out these frozen logs.

These mushrooms are notorious for showing up right after major snow storms, especially in January, where the next day after a cold snap the protruding body of the mushrooms can be seen. These mushrooms are usually fairly easy to spot, their color ranges from all white mushroom caps to a more grey sheen that is perpetrated by extreme frost. These mushrooms have a great savory taste and make for some wonderful stir fry along with a few other choice wild foods.

Wintergreen

This is a wild food that not only survives the winter season, it thrives in it. This plant is a very low creeping plant and is an acidic specimen of the heath genus. The Wintergreen is typically found in the mountains, and is most especially abundant throughout the Canadian Shied. The leaves are minty and are a great supplement raw and also a good beverage in your tea or coffee.

As you may have realized this minty fresh additive natural for the wintergreen plant is also used in quite a few modern items such as chewing gum, candy, and even toothpaste. This wild food typically spreads itself out from under the soil with its spear like roots clinging to particles of dead plant matter such as leaves bark and sticks, with their leaves fully ripening in the dead of winter.

Chapter 5: How to Store your Wild Food All Year Long

Ok, so far in this book we have covered our 15 wild foods, discussing at great length about what to look for, where to find them, and what they are good for. Now in this chapter we are going to take a look at what you should do after you find your supply of wild foods. We're going to learn how we can make the best of our finds and store them for a very long time.

First up in our discussion, we are going to take a look at a type of food storage center that has been with us for a very long time. Your grandma probably had one and you didn't even know about it, as these forage storage centers were usually hidden away in basements or outside under the ground. What kind of food storing facility am I talking about? Why the Root Cellar of course!

Hailing from England sometime in the 17th century, the concept of storing food in a cold dark, deep place, taking advantage of the natural refrigeration of the Earth, soon became the norm in the rest of the world as well. As a result, in North America, constructing houses with a built in Root Cellar became standard fair.

It was only in the early 20th century when electric refrigerators began to become more common place, that the Root Cellar starting to wane in its importance. But the Root Cellar should not be dismissed it still has several distinct advantages when it come to storing food, especially wild, foraged food. In fact, it has been well documented that produce such as, cucumbers, eggplant cauliflower, and their wild food variations do much better in an actual root cellar than in a refrigerator.

Many of these veggies will be soggy and damp after a month in a typical modern refrigerator, but in the more natural environment of a root cellar they can last much longer. A well insulated cellar can keep the food inside up to 40 degrees cooler than they would be if they were outside during the summer months and during the winter the root cellar is able to keep produce at just above freezing, greatly slowing down the degradation of your produce.

A proper root cellar can be easily requisitioned in an unused corner of a basement or even just by digging a pit outside. To construct a basement root cellar all you have to do is wall off the corner of your basement that is facing the northernmost wall. Pressure treated stud walls work best for this, and are easy to install and easy to remove when you need to take them out.

Within the corner of your root cellar also try to put down some wooden slats so that you will have a raised platform on which to put your produce. Then just make sure that you keep a thermometer near a vent or window so that you can keep track of the internal temperature of the cellar. After doing this, you are good to go, and can begin storing your produce within your root cellar.

If you don't have a basement however, another good food storage option for you is that of the "Root-Pit" basically the same idea as any other root cellar—which works to take advantage of the natural coolness of the Earth—except a lot more basic. Because this wild food storage concept is so down to earth that it takes us into the earth itself!

All you have to do is dig about six feet into the ground and then drop down a layer of leaves for bedding. After you have put your layer of leaf bedding down you can then start stacking up your crates (or whatever container you use) of wild foods on top of each other down inside the hole.

Now just take another layer of leaves and cover the top of your produce with them. Once you have done this bury the whole thing in about 5 inches of dirt. Burying food is an ancient storage practice, taking produce back to the earth from whence they came. So if you are out foraging in the great outdoors with nowhere else to pack your veggies don't look any further than the ground beneath your feet!

Along with improvised refrigeration, another thing that you should keep in mind when you are trying to store your produce is what kind of containers to put them in. Many resort to store bought plastic bags and Tupperware which in the long run, give mixed results at best. Just keep in mind that the main thing that you need to be concerned with when you are storing the wild food that you have foraged is the level of moisture within the environment and within the produce itself.

You don't want so little moisture that the food shrivels and dries up, but you also don't won't so much moisture that the food starts to attract mold and rot. Maintaining a proper amount of moisture is the key for any storage practices you will undertake. Having that said, plastic bags are to be avoided since they don't allow for the right amount of air to be able to circulate, and ultimately will result in some rather slimy, inedible foods.

So rather than sealing things up in Ziploc tight bags you should always use some sort of perforated containers that will allow for circulation. Wild berries especially must be kept in storage units that allow for them to breathe. Because completely sealed up, these foods will turn into a moldy mess in no time.

The best thing you can do for your berries is to rinse them off after you pick them and then let them dry out completely before you store them. I usually leave mine out in the sun for a day or so, letting nature do its work for me, making sure that they are completely dry. Once this has been achieved you can then take your berries and put them in your perforated container.

Drying is another great method for wild foods and herbs. This is a method that entails literally hanging your foraged bounty out to dry in order to preserve their freshness. All you have to do is take some elastic bands and use them to tie your plant stems into small bundles and then find a nice dry place away from direct sunlight. And then hang them upside down so that they can naturally dry themselves out, getting rid of any excess moisture that they have within them.

If you are dealing with several plants at once, just make sure that you keep your bundles fairly small and space them evenly apart as you leave them out to dry. Elastic bands are ideal for this exercise because they can adjust their grip on the plant as their moisture evaporates and they begin to slightly shrink in size. If you are indoors, an unused corner of the house away from direct exposure to your windows works just fine.

And if you are outdoors you can get the same effect simply by hanging them up on a branch of a shade tree. They key is to allow them to slowly dry from the warmth of the day, without being completely blasted by direct sunlight. After your wild foods have finished drying you can then gather them up and store them in any container you wish. This way you can store all the great wild foods you have foraged all year long.

Conclusion: Any Season of the Year

There is nothing quite like the feeling of pride that is instilled when you can learn how to be self reliant and do something for yourself. Independence is something that most of us desperately crave yet in every aspect of our mass production society; we have become more dependent than ever before. This is why people are so excited to learn about ways that they can at least temporarily unplug themselves from the grid that has been engineered and instituted all around us. And learn how to do something that is completely unbidden and un-beholden to anyone else.

The only reason that I ever went on my own foray into the wilderness to forage for food was because a friend of mine who is an all out nature nut and fitness enthusiasts convinced me to go hiking with him one weekend. This go was an ex-marine and a prepper survivalist to the extreme. Little did I know that this one simple hiking trip would turn into our very own episode of survivor!

The trouble started when we somehow found ourselves off the beaten path and completely lost in a labyrinth of overgrown hiking trails. Being in this wild terrain longer than expected the meager supplies I had brought with me were gone in no time. Low on water and with no food I started to flip out. But my friend whipping out his inner MacGyver knew what to do.

He started pointing out wild mushrooms and foliage that we could eat until we found our way back to camp. And suffice it to say, we didn't starve, and we made it back the next day, not only in good health, but with a new awareness of just how fulfilling living off the land can be. This was the episode that kick started my own enthusiasm for foraging, a passion that now sticks with me any season of the year.

FREE Bonus Reminder

If you have not grabbed it yet, please go ahead and download your
special bonus report *"Leptin Resistance. 21 Leptin Recipes For Weight
Loss & Healthy Living"*.
Simply Click the Button Below

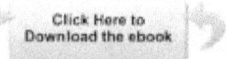

OR **Go to This Page**
http://easyweightlossway.com/free/

BONUS #2: More Free & Discounted Books
Do you want to receive more Free & Discounted Books?
We have a mailing list where we send out our new Books when they go free or with a discount on Kindle. Click on the link below to sign up for Free & Discount Book Promotions.
=> Sign Up for Free & Discount Book Promotions <=

OR Go to this URL
http://zbit.ly/1WBb1Ek